OUR LIFE

Craig Newnes is a consulting conversationalist, editor, dad, grandad, musician, author, cook and gardener. Until retiring after a near-fatal road accident, he was director of one of England's largest National Health Service Psychological Therapies Departments. He has published many chapters and academic articles and is editor of *The Journal of Critical Psychology, Counselling and Psychotherapy*. He was, for 19 years, the editor of *Clinical Psychology Forum*, the journal of the Division of Clinical Psychology of the British Psychological Society. He has been an Honorary Professor in Australia and an Honorary Lecturer in clinical psychology at several UK universities. He now practices Compassionate Conversation via a barter system. He has received two Human Rights awards for over thirty years of speaking out about harm caused by psychology and psychiatry. His books include *Clinical Psychology: A critical examination* from PCCS Books and *Inscription, Diagnosis and Deception in the Mental Health Industry: How Psy governs us all,* from Palgrave Macmillan. *A Critical A-Z of Electroshock* was published in 2018 by the Real Press as well as a children's book, *The Billy and Bonzo Stories*.

52 WAYS to change your LIFE

Craig Newnes

THE REAL PRESS
www.therealpress.co.uk

Published in 2019 by the Real Press.
www.therealpress.co.uk

Print ISBN 9781912119851
Ebook ISBN 9781912119844

To Isabel – who changed everything.

Acknowledgements

As ever, thanks to David Boyle and my indulgent family.

I am indebted to some remarkably loyal friends; Kevin, Steve, Jules and Julia and to a fair few no longer with us, especially Dorothy Rowe, Ron Cattrall, Osman Shouli and David Smail.

Chapters

Introduction

SOME of the best things in life may be free. Many are accidental. This volume began with a road accident, an accident that killed a good friend and left me in a coma for two weeks. It was just before Christmas in 2003, my partner Isabel was seven months pregnant and, as director of an acclaimed department of Psychological Therapies in the National Health Service, I thought myself a pretty lucky guy – all hubris of course.

Helicoptered to an intensive care unit in Birmingham, I entered a world of myth and magic. We had been to see the third part of *The Lord of the Rings* the night before and I was surrounded by orcs, monsters too various to name and a blackness that came and went. Hooked up to tubes and devices draining fluid from the brain, pumped full of anaesthetic and adrenaline to maintain unconsciousness, all seemed lost.

On Christmas Eve, my brother was told by the consultant that I wouldn't last 24 hours. His response? 'We need a second opinion here!'

Crushed sternum, punctured lung, three brain haematomae, fractured vertebra, twisted spinal cord, half severed brachial plexus, four broken ribs – the list goes on. After a few weeks, the number of times relatives who had been informed that 'He's the luckiest man alive' went into double figures.

So, many moons later, I sat down to write a list of the kind of things that may have contributed to this luck. Perhaps, 'A Hundred Ways to Live Forever' was a little over the top. And, in any case, the list only reached sixty-four, however many attempts were made. The list also excluded accidental influences – like being Jewish, white, male, happening to have an accident only a helicopter journey away from life-saving staff and technology and so many other aspects we call context. Then, taking a leaf (and several pages) out of my own book, I quit while I was ahead and stopped at fifty-two, rather neatly one for each week of the year that will change your life.

What you have before you, then, is the edited list with a coda adding some extras, extras that have sustained this weary body for another fifteen years. The body would have been, coincidentally, sixty-four, but this has taken a while longer than expected. You may already do some, or many, of the fifty-two ways. If you want to change your life, I suggest you take five new ones at random and see if you can maintain them.

As the notes make clear, maintaining new conduct is so much harder than changing ingrained habits. I wish you luck.

The Ways

1. Get rid of your TV.
2. If you don't really love the person you are living with as a partner, leave.
3. If you're on a diet to lose weight, get off it.
4. Learn to cook.
5. Grow house plants.
6. Work out what so-called news is promoting.
7. Read at least two Dickens novels (as an adult).
8. Read *Lord of the Rings* at least three times.
9. Take the barest minimum of prescription drugs.
10. Grow vegetables and eat them.
11. Betray a principle.

12. See 'A Clockwork Orange' and 'Mary Poppins'.
13. Swear a lot.
14. Vote for a political party that's demonstrably egalitarian.
15. Only advise people to do things that you're able to do yourself
16. Be a step-parent or foster a child.
17. Appreciate the glory of the night sky.
18. Have children with the person you love.
19. Shout when you're angry.
20. Always wear comfortable clothes.
21. Masturbate regularly.
22. Live with several different people, including a Jew and a Catholic.
23. Don't bother with underwear.
24. Go fishing and decide for yourself if it's cruel.
25. Know that so-called psy experts make it up as they go along.
26. Write something every day.
27. Respond to letters and other correspondence.
28. Send greetings cards more haphazardly.
29. Play a musical instrument at least five hours per week.
30. Don't try to be liked.

31. Celebrate friendship.
32. Search out solidarity.
33. Run, swim or cycle and play something competitive (cards will do).
34. Do as many chores as you can when going from one end of where you live to the other.
35. Use ordinary words, not technical labels, to describe how people behave.
36. Avoid physical fights.
37. Don't make happiness an ambition.
38. Live somewhere for ten or more years.
39. Eat by candlelight regularly.
40. Spend time with someone who is very, very ill with cancer.
41. Be on time for people in and out of work.
42. Alternate between the main newspapers – but focus on the cryptic crossword.
43. Join a club.
44. Eat lots of garlic.
45. If someone hurts you badly, run a long, long way.
46. Look after a dog, or dogs, for many years.
47. Support your local community.
48. When you smoke dope, inhale.
49. Forgive your father.
50. Learn to drive.

51. Learn a foreign language and live in a country other than that of your birth.
52. Visit the Great Blasket.

One

Get rid of your TV

Sounds easy doesn't it? I haven't owned a television for over forty years but it was no great moral choice to pass it on. In the middle of a marriage break-up, we took turns opting for furnishings, cassette recordings and the rest. All very civilised; marriages and divorces tend to go the same way as the relationship – if you have been friends, the separation will be reasonable; if you have previously been at loggerheads, you will need a solicitor.

Liz opted for the television and I never got round to replacing it. Rather like giving up cigarettes, the first few days are likely to be the worst. After a few weeks, I couldn't remember why I had looked forward to *Dallas*.

People are appalled at the suggestion: 'I'd have to *talk* to my husband instead of reading while he watches the sport!', 'What about the poor children? You're denying them!' And so on. But just think – no so-called news, no nonsense from badly dressed politicians being beamed into your living space, none of those adverts for toys that have the kids clamouring in early September for *the* Christmas present.

Two

If you don't really love the person you are living with as a partner, leave

I know, I know. Easier said than done. After all, the person you are living with might be violent and threatening, or you might both be embroiled in a joint mortgage or renting a place you can't afford alone and so on. And it's easy to get stuck on what notions of 'love' might be. As a psychotherapist I saw plenty of women living with apparently vicious partners who sometimes acknowledged that separation was too scary/ complicated/ time-consuming/ expensive/ whatever, but also occasionally said: 'I can't leave him, I love him.'

It was a position reinforced by friends and family who occasionally said things like: 'I can't see what she sees in him', only to get the response: 'She must love him.' For these witnesses, love wasn't so much blind as a kind of fog obscuring reality. Whatever else, love is deaf – getting bawled at in the early hours for having the temerity to have gone out the evening before requires phantom ear-plugs.

It was easier for me – male, employed, knowing that my wife (female, employed) would easily find someone else if she wanted (she did – three times). We were also child-less and living in a rented house so only bound by genuine affection and friendship. I fell for someone else, told my wife and that was it really – apart from splitting up the chattels (see Get Rid of Your TV).

Years later, I thought I knew something of love: 'Falling in love isn't in your control, Beatriz. It's a wonderfully accurate phrase, isn't it? You fall, with amazing luck, you both fall into it. It's like a bottomless, heavenly well. You both tumble, then plunge. Down and down. Holding hands, hearts – whatever comes to hand (a grin – mother really is quite something). I know you know this. But luck never holds you, Beatriz. One day, one of you hits the side of the well. The other keeps falling, always hurting – I almost said hearting. Knowing your souls are no longer bound, no longer one in this life. That somewhere, far above you, lies the broken body that can only be touched now in dreams.'[1]

Three
If you're on a diet to lose weight, get off it

My mum was on a diet, on and off, for about sixty years and was three times the Heinz 'Slimmer of the Month.' In those six decades, she lost around three tonnes in weight – and put on about three tonnes and forty pounds. A few months eating little while confined to hospital and a nursing home in her late eighties and her weight dropped to forty kilogrammes.

You may be Olympics or Tour de France material and chucking down vast quantities of carbohydrates to burn off in the pool or on the road. You may well be a chronic dieter or possibly just a faddist. But, I ask you – what's it all *for*?

Perhaps it's to fit into that dress you bought in the sales, perhaps you really are training for a half marathon. I did six full marathons, one of which – Boston – was completed after a six-month intake of little but egg rolls and bourbon. Asked what I was running away from when training began a few years earlier, one possible answer was 'fat'. But fat wasn't an issue. Hurt was the issue. People are hurt all the time and a constant critical self-commentary on our physique driven by advertising, magazines and stereotypic beauty in the media leads people to diet and then eat for 'comfort'. If they gain weight, the obvious thing to do is to carry on eating but to eat 'healthily'.

The outcome is a Northern Hemisphere obsessed with diet – and second hand bookshops filled with unopened diet books and discarded cook books.

Do yourself a favour – if you have already dieted, put diets on a diet. Bet you can.

Four
Learn to cook

Inspiration has many sources. Grandmothers (especially Jewish matriarchs) have a sacred place in the lives of lucky grand-children. Part of that reputation comes from their cooking – often plain, frequently plentiful, the food served up with real pleasure. If your parents aren't much cop at cooking, and a grandmother or two not readily available, you may have to learn to cook.

Remember *Vesta* curries? De-hydrated, enough for two or four depending on budget and quickly prepared to be served with a jar of an equally exotic mango chutney. Popular in the 1960s, they seemed a sure-fire way to conjure up an Eastern feast. Aged fourteen, I prepared one for the then love of my life. Drambuie was the accompanying tipple as the Newnes family didn't do wine (or beer for that matter). It was a disaster.

Jung claimed that we *only* learn from our own mistakes (it is humankind's loss that we don't learn from other people's). So – no more *Vesta*. Instead, a half century of learning how to cook. Like playing an instrument or making love, practice leads to improvement if not perfection. Practice also leads to creativity, knowing the most flavoursome combinations and, if you are lucky, to a degree of approbation.

Here's a tip; if you want a low salt diet, just use your usual recipes and leave out the salt, as it happens, another key to a pretty healthy life.

Elizabeth David introduced a post-rationing Britain to a different style of home cookery in 1950 via *A Book of Mediterranean Food.* Notwithstanding the difficulty of getting hold of olive oil and recipes that involved up to twelve eggs, the book remains a tribute to her trust in British cooks – there are few explanations of cookery terms and oven temperatures are pretty vague. It's all about experimentation.

And if cooking seems too much trouble try this: *For exceptionally busy mums. The best way to prepare this dish is to get your partner to mix the Martini and do all the food preparation too. If you want, you might like to entertain each other in the kitchen a little. This will depend on what you are wearing but a basque is to be recommended.*[1]

Five
Grow house plants

If you want to get all squishy about it, I'd say that many of the fifty two ways are about celebrating life – itself something of a change for many. *Surrounding* yourself with life (and oxygen releasing greenery) is harder than you might think if you don't do it already. Sorry – another change that turns out to be difficult. Tough, even.

The shortest way into growing house-plants is to ask for one from a friend who knows what they are doing (feeding at the right time, not over-watering, re-potting, finding the best light, etc) and then follow their advice. You might – sadly – kill a few but, if re-positioning doesn't work, try a different plant. Don't worry too much about flowering plants (although the tiny white flowers on spider plants are pretty) – the aim is to fill spaces with living greenery; colour is a bonus you can move onto later.

How much later? Get ready for spending at least six months before you feel remotely proficient at keeping plants going. Like any habit, the habit of checking soil dampness, root bound-ness and the rest takes time to bed in.

Six

Work out what so called news is promoting

This isn't so difficult though it requires the development of a certain amount of cynicism. Being cynical has changed in meaning from its early origins as a philosophy of seeing things as they are (uncomfortable though that might be) to a disparagement of a person – someone is now described as cynical if they remark that, for example, politicians are self-serving or that companies use tropes like 'health' to sell their products.

Of course, that's exactly what companies do – from producing 'healthy' energy drinks to 'healthy' alternatives to meat for vegetarians. Plant-based foods might well be better for you and the planet in the long run but cynical (in the old sense of the word) advertising just uses whatever the promotional currency of the day is in order to sell.

One moment, a product is better for your

liver/heart/digestion and the next it's better for the ozone layer or 'future generations'. Rather like the mass production of all those hybrid vehicles that will cut down on carbon: it is estimated that the manufacture of a new car uses the carbon equivalent of twenty years motoring in an existing vehicle.

'News' has fallen into the promotional bracket since Leni Riefenstahl directed the Nazi propaganda films *Triumph des Willens* ('Triumph of the Will') and *Olympia* in the 1930s. America and Britain joined in with their own propaganda exercises in the Second World War and so-called news hasn't changed much since. We are taught that it *matters* that a member of the royal family is pregnant/ill/visiting an estate in Scotland or that a television personality has written about an unremarkable event in their childhood (for serialisation/a new autobiography or whatever) or that there has been a 'breakthrough' in dementia treatment (in an experiment involving 150 *mice*).

To an extent, it's all entertainment. To a greater extent, it's advertising the existence of the royal family or the publication of the autobiography or the name of the research team hungry for continued funding. You may already suspect that the news is biased. It is quite possible to see it as irrelevant but that requires cynicism …

Seven
Read at least two Dickens novels (as an adult)

Why Dickens? Why not Balzac, Hugo, Sartre, or Zola? My guess is that, unless you are French, you weren't expected to read Balzac *et al*, as a child but, if you did, by all means go back to the nineteenth century giants and have another bash. Balzac, in particular, can hold new meaning if you have a mortgage based on a bank's or building society's usury or if you have credit card debt up to your eyeballs.

In nineteenth century France, the petit bourgeoisie were held to ransom by money-lenders, which may not have meant very much to you as a twentieth century teenager, but will seem horribly familiar now. Balzac's *Comedie Humaine* exhaustively covers the misery of debt.

Dickens though… The cult of celebrity might be said to originate with Charles Dickens who read and performed to hundreds in specially hired halls. His first readings were for charity, beginning with two performances of *A Christmas Carol* in front of 2,000 working-class people in Birmingham. The author turned professional performer in 1858. Between December 1867 and April 1868, he earned over £19,000 (the equivalent of almost a million pounds today).

You may well have, at the very least, read *A Christmas Carol* or *David Copperfield* as a child. Seen through an adult's eyes, the likes of *Bleak House, Hard Times* or *Oliver Twist* bring angst and poverty alive in a way that is palpable. You might even find some sympathy for Bill Sikes.

Criticizing Dickens for his overwhelmingly male cast of characters and some pretty stereotypically pathetic women rather misses the strength of Mrs Cratchit or the courage of Nancy; at least as an adult reader you can judge for yourself. You might even suggest *Oliver Twist* to a book club (see Join a club).

Eight
Read Lord of the Rings at least three times

Perhaps you've read it. Perhaps twice? It's a big book – not as big as *War and Peace,* one volume I might suggest you don't try – but re-reading literary works is important. Books tell you a lot about who you are at any given moment – the meaning you get from them changes over time. I could suggest any number of re-read volumes – from the viciously humorous Tom Sharpe to the mordant, sometimes crazy, worlds of Iris Murdoch or Mervyn Peake.

How does reading and re-reading change your life? It's not so different from learning to play an instrument. It takes time; the more you do of it, the less time you have for other things (watching television, walking the dog, phoning your mum …) so, again by definition, your life changes. If you have already ditched your TV (Number One), then you will have more than enough time to walk the dog or phone your mum a*nd* have a bash at Tolkein.

Nine

Take the barest minimum of prescription drugs

Any prescribed medication has adverse effects. For marketing purposes, these are called 'side effects.' But one person's adverse effect is another person's desired outcome – drugs prescribed for so-called Attention Deficit Hyperactivity Disorder (ADHD) are a form of speed. Too much speed slows you down – handy for an over-worked parent or teacher with a rambunctious seven-year-old climbing the walls.

Speed also decreases appetite and we are probably only months away from drug companies promoting this so called adverse effect as a good thing in a campaign marketing *Adderall* or *Ritalin* as *slimming* pills.

Effexor (Venlafaxine) is a regularly prescribed so called anti-depressant. Venlafaxine is known as a serotonin-norepinephrine reuptake inhibitor (SNRI). The listed adverse effects are (commonly), lack or loss of strength, severe headache and sweating. Not so bad you might think. According to the manufacturer's leaflet, however, less common adverse effects include blurred vision, chest pain, fast or irregular heartbeat, mood or mental changes, ringing or buzzing in the ears and suicidal thoughts (ironic in an anti-depressant, but commoner than you might suppose as SNRIs lead to agitation and that can be unbearable).

It gets worse; other effects are: actions that are out of control, convulsions, high fever, irritability, itching or skin rash, light-headedness or fainting, especially when getting up suddenly from a sitting or lying position, menstrual changes, nervousness (odd, some prescribers recommend Effexor to people who are anxious), problems with urinating or holding urine, severe muscle stiffness, talking, feeling, and acting with excitement that you cannot control (more agitation), trouble breathing and unusually pale skin.

The incidence of the following is not known: loss of libido, bloody, light-coloured, black, or tarry stools, dark, bloody and decreased frequency or amount of urine, diarrhoea, drowsiness and a general feeling of tiredness or weakness, fever and increased thirst, muscle cramps, spasms, or pain, nausea or vomiting, nosebleeds, overactive reflexes, poor co-ordination, red or purple spots on the skin, restlessness, shivering, stomach pain on the upper right side, swelling of the face, lower legs, ankles, hands, or fingers, hard to control trembling, shaking and twitching, unusual bruising, unusual tiredness or weakness, vomiting of blood or material that looks like coffee grounds and yellow eyes or skin.

The list of potential interactions (contra-indications) with other drugs taken simultaneously with *Effexor* beggars belief.[1]

Add in the impact of drinking coffee, alcohol, sugar-free drinks, whatever and the combinations of interaction become too complicated to estimate.

In addition, the adverse effect reporting mechanism is deeply flawed. It isn't possible to know how many people suffer a loss of libido, agitation and the rest because once a general practitioner has reported an effect on the yellow forms at the back of the *British National Formulary*[2] it is included in the list – and once it's there, a busy practitioner won't feel they need to report it again.

Effexor wasn't chosen at random but because it is so commonly prescribed. But any prescribed medication will have various adverse effects, some of which will be far worse than the condition they are meant to treat and others will *produce* the condition for which they are prescribed.

So, take the barest minimum. And, if you are on a psychiatric drug, get help to wean yourself off it.

Ten

Grow vegetables and eat them

A mate lives six storeys up a tower block in central London. Leaning over the balcony, you can see Petticoat Lane and banker types wandering along it. Less than twenty metres directly opposite is a fifty odd storey office building with blue tinted glass and internal lighting that never seems to go off. And yet, every summer on that shaded balcony, there is a thriving tomato plant.

At a pinch, he could add oregano, garlic and welsh onion (they dangle from stalks) plants and *voilà*! He has the makings of a decent Italian sauce.

In some ways, growing vegetables is also about celebrating life (see Grow House Plants) but there's more to it than that. If you happen to have a small garden not too shaded by trees and buildings, then you have the makings of that essential of the vegetable gardener's life – the compost heap.

Stand a wooden pallet on its side to create a space about a metre wide in a sunny corner of the plot. Instead of throwing peelings, old envelopes, cardboard cereal packaging and the rest into the recycling bin, chuck it into the compost space and watch it fill. You can cover it after six months and – in another six months – you can use it.

Don't worry, you don't have to wait six months for the life-changing growing of veg. You can start with spuds in any old soil – just make sure you get a local veg grower to help you sort out the bewildering number of available tubers; first earlies, second earlies, main-crop etc, etc. Rather nicely, there's the preparatory phase of 'chitting' to go through first – no need to go outside at all, just put the seed potatoes (you can use spuds bought from a supermarket if they have vestigial 'eyes') in an aired basket, wait a few weeks and when the eyes are inch-long stalks, plant 'em.

You can plant in your beautifully prepared soil, barely dug soil or a soil-filled bucket. You'll have to wait three months before you eat them – after the flowers have finished and the greenery has died right down – so there's plenty of time to crack on with the artichoke, asparagus and chard beds … Maybe next year.

Eleven
Betray a principle

Another tricky one, this. If you want to be psychological about it then many of the fifty-two ways are what family therapists describe as first-order changes. They don't require a fundamental shift in values or a – possibly – unarticulated guiding philosophy. They're still far from easy – have you ever *tried* to play a musical instrument for at least five hours a week (Number 29)?

A second order change is something else again and usually brought about by events rather than what the world calls choice, for example, falling in love. Betrayal can be deliberate; if you read spy novels, you'll get the picture. More often it comes through changes you make that go against a (second order) principle you have previously held dear. That principle may well be embodied in the strictures of religion and custom or the words of wisdom from an admired, even beloved, relative or family icon.

So in, for example, leaving a partner to be with someone you love (Number Two) you may be betraying a parent who had told you that 'marriage - like a dog - is for life, not just for Christmas'. Along the way, you may have betrayed your partner (hardly uncommon as two thirds of marriages end in divorce, a separation that often follows years of strife, disharmony or affairs) justifying your conduct on the basis that love is a higher principle than your marriage vows.

For marriage, Harold Pinter's play *Betrayal* says it all. Written in 1978 during an affair with Antonia Fraser who he subsequently married, the play is about the lies and self-deception Pinter experienced during a previous affair with the journalist Joan Bakewell.

It reveals not only the simpler aspects of first-order change typical of affairs (staying out 'unexpectedly', lying to your partner and so on) but also the second-order change necessary in such betrayals – being forced to see yourself as flawed, dishonest, human...

For a woman going out alone was, for many years, a sign of being a disreputable person and in the nineteenth century for middle class women, the possibility that you were a harlot or, worse still, independent. For many women taught, in the last century, that their role was 'in the home' going to the cinema alone was a betrayal of the prime directive and those (parents, priests) who had delivered it.

So be aware that many of these ways to change involve a betrayal, not just of the person you have seen yourself as but as the person you have been told to be by people who claim to have had your best interests in mind.

Betraying someone isn't an option if you follow a new way of being.

Twelve
See 'A Clockwork Orange' and 'Mary Poppins'

Kubrick is a phenomenon – try *Barry Lyndon* (I wouldn't bother with *Eyes Wide Shut*). *A Clockwork Orange* has it all – disgusting violence, extraordinary acting, Beethoven's Ninth. But why the recommendation? I saw it – at Bexhill's Delaware Pavilion of all places – when it first appeared, and before Kubrick withdrew it soon after critics had lambasted it and some Tory grandees and good Christians had branded it obscene.

Tarantino has long since topped the violence and, no doubt, similar grandees and Christians scour the internet for porn in order to check on modern day obscenity levels (they're high). So it's not about the violence or the gruesome rape scene. It's partly about seeing something you suspect will be upsetting and partly about – well, you will have to find out for yourself.

Now for *Mary Poppins;* Dick van Dyke's shining

hour (almost topped by his appearance in *Mary Poppins Two*). We love magic – electricity is magic (something we don't understand) to many of us. Psy professionals claim a kind of magic (understanding people) and many offer something even more extraordinary – transformation through chatting with an 'expert.'

This book is more grounded. It offers change, but not through magic; through doing things differently or for the first time, or not at all. None of that's easy as you will soon discover. But watching a movie? What could be easier than that?

The deal is, you must watch it from the opening to the closing credits and then think about what part was most touching, hilarious, meaningful and, well, magical. That's it. Your reactions might mirror some of my own (even though I first saw *Mary Poppins* when it first came out and have seen it many times since) but it doesn't matter. What counts is the *conversations* you can have with others about the experience.

Better than talking about climate change …

Thirteen
Swear a lot

This relates to Nineteen (Shout when you're angry) with a none-too-subtle difference. Both exercises are about letting off steam – the steam of frustration clogs rather than clears the pores. Swearing has a moral element that renders it – in that most pompous of expressions – 'inappropriate' in polite company. And G-d forbid that you be inappropriate and less than polite.

Being polite is something of a curse. It silences sub-ordinates and can leave us at the mercy of powerful (by virtue of class) others. Even starting a conversation can be positioned as impolite by our 'elders and betters' and interrupting or contradicting a speaker is likely to be seen as rude. Imagine that, being rude …

Which brings us to swearing. As a ceiling tiler, I worked with a guy from Walthamstow in North East London. Marvellously, his name really was Del. And Del from Walthamstow knew how to swear. His use of the best-known Anglo-Saxon profanity was like a form of punctuation combined with a verbal tic; to such an extent he was able to put more f^{xxx}s into a sentence than all the other words.

Billy Connolly was a notorious user of the F word. He once explained at the beginning of a show, however, that the audience was likely to misunderstand him as the word he was actually using was *fucque* – apparently a Thai word meaning … I can't remember what (I was laughing too hard to hear the definition).

The moral dimension combined with the demand to be polite makes swearing a minefield and thus, a fantastic opportunity. Religions, customs and codes the world over make swearing something to be avoided. Perhaps you swear already. Good onya – go on to Number Fourteen. Perhaps you don't. Now's the time to learn – watch a couple of Tarantino films for instruction, though it can be hard to distinguish the swearing from violence. Just don't shoot anyone.

Fourteen
Vote for a political party that's demonstrably egalitarian

How, you might ask, did politics get in here? The best kind of politics – and a form this author followed until a kind of resigned cynicism took over – involves following an ideal. If your ideal is outright individualism, then it might be time to shift to a more collectivist stance. Being demonstrably egalitarian is much easier for a party *en bloc* than any individual Member of Parliament.

Workers in the North Shropshire Labour Party, for example, found themselves campaigning for a candidate who was an Oxford-educated lawyer and far removed from the agricultural or unemployed electorate of much of the constituency. He didn't get in and was moved on to a 'safe' seat. Not long after, the party went full circle in the individualism stakes and issued membership cards emblazoned with photographs of the new leader (Tony Blair).

Time to resign – but English men didn't get the

vote until the late 1800s and women not until the 1920s and it's not something to be ignored. So vote, and vote for a party that is demonstrably egalitarian.

Fifteen
Don't suggest others do what you can't do yourself

The dictum 'Don't suggest others do what you can't do yourself – they might need some back-up' can be found on various powerpoint (sorry) slides used with professional groups over many years. In part, it's a dig at people recommending therapy when they have never experienced it as a patient. Mostly, it's about the simpler notion that people find advice in equal parts infuriating and impossible to follow unless they have support from someone who has 'been there, done that'.

This volume is testament to the dictum. None of the fifty two ways were plucked out of the air (though, see Coda). Instead, they are real, achievable and – if you want some help – you know who to ask.

Number Fifteen has the advantage of avoiding what is said to be the first lesson – hypocrisy. You know the scene – a mum screams at her daughter,

'How many times have I told you to stop shouting.' It's 'do as I say not as I do.'

Number Fifteen avoids that. It's 'I've done this, do you want a hand?'

Sixteen

Be a step-parent or foster a child

For many, step-parenting is a different beast to looking after your own children. There may be another parent out there somewhere with a claim or a parent who has died. You are left to cope with your step-child's disappointment that you can't live up to an idealised version of being a mum or dad or that same step-child's relief and pleasure that you are a) still alive and b) pretty good at your new role.

Parent-hood takes considerable adjustment (see Have a child with someone that you love) and step-parenthood requires all sorts of manoeuvring. It will change you. No guarantees here, as it's another human being you are taking into the fold and human beings can be insufferable, entertaining, unkind, pompous, fun to be with, all of the richness that comes with relationship.

But there's a crunch – like having a child of your own, you don't get the chance to give it back, so step-parenting is a one-time deal. Not for the feint hearted.

Fostering has its own complications. Working as a consultant psychologist, I once supervised a group of social workers involved in supporting foster families all living in the same town. Several of the families fostered more than one child, each of whom had a different social worker. Remarkably, for 'reasons of confidentiality', social workers in the group had agreed amongst themselves not to offer opinions on the work of colleagues when they knew the family under discussion by virtue of their relationship with a different child in the family.

In effect, each family had an extended professional family (which might involve counsellors, general practitioners and psychiatrists) who didn't speak to each other about shared concerns when given the opportunity.

As a potential foster parent you will also be expected to undergo a series of interviews to check for 'suitability', potential for violence, etc. Having your own child requires no such testing, nor does becoming a step-parent. Neither is easy, but change isn't meant to be...

Seventeen
Appreciate the glory of the night sky

On the 'Forward Planner 1979' page of a 1978 diary (see Write something every day), in capital letters. there are five words written through February, March, April May and June: LIVE FOR MOST OF IT. This volume is mostly about appreciating being alive – however shit things might seem for a while.

Gardening, looking after house plants, dogs or children are all life-giving (if sometimes draining) ways to be. But stars are a whole other story.

The night sky is simultaneously fabulous and a reminder of what specks of dust we all are. So, beware of taking yourself too seriously. A flight across any ocean or large country can have the same impact – it takes five hours to cross either the Indian Ocean or China at 600 miles per hour and four to cross Australia (which looks like a vast expanse of nothing but red from 30,000 feet up). None of the people on islands or boats in the ocean or on the ground below know that you exist – nor, probably ever will.

So, you see, this one is about getting perspective. Number Thirty One was going to be 'Remind yourself that, for everyone who applauds your success, there will be someone who hates you for it and countless others who will never even know you exist.' It seemed a bit wordy and appreciating the night sky has a more positive feel don't you think?

But – like the overwhelming majority of the world, the stars just don't *care a*bout you. They are simply glorious and distant. Be grateful.

Eighteen
Have children with the person you love

This has a number of disadvantages. For a start, if you are trying one suggestion per week, this one will take a bit longer. This book will be long forgotten before you change the first nappy – as might be your partner and the reasons you thought it such a good idea at the time.

Children are hard work, get in the way (a friend used to say that the worst thing people who love each other can do is to have a child – the child will feel excluded) and the so-called 'Terrible Twos' soon go on to the 'Terrifying Threes', the 'Fearsome Fours', 'Frustrating Fives' – on and on until you get to the moment when the youngest wants to borrow your car or the eldest insists on moving back in, having found independence too expensive.

Billy Connolly used to say that 'We're here to have babies and look after the place.' Who am I to disagree with the Scottish Sage? You want to change your life? This one should do it …

Nineteen
Shout when you're angry

Being a runner helped – people around Slough and later Harvard must have been taken aback when the jogger training for his next marathon suddenly yelled out loud.

All of us get angry. You can bottle it, express it by bursting into tears, take it out on someone else … human beings are really inventive when it comes to not just letting go. So, shout – don't mind the neighbours, they'll soon knock on the dividing wall.

Twenty
Always wear comfortable clothes

Samuel Bentham was working as an overseer in Krichev (white Russia, now Belarus) when visited by his brother, Jeremy, in the late 1780s. His suggestion – a circular building as the hub of a larger factory where unskilled workers could be observed by a few managers – was taken up by Jeremy Bentham as a model for prisons.

Named the *panopticon*, the concept included the notion that prisoners would not know when their cell was being watched and would begin to monitor each other to make sure their own cell group wasn't punished. Bentham described the panopticon as 'a new mode of obtaining power of mind over mind.'[1]

The panopticon is with us all the time now, either via CCTV cameras that may or may not be working or through a perpetual self-monitoring: 'Am I looking good / behaving properly / too loud / too quiet ...?'

‘Looking good’ can be more important than actually getting fit for runners and cyclists sporting the latest lycra. ‘Looking good’ can seriously impede comfort when it comes to clothing. Some companies still have ‘casual’ days when employees are not expected to wear ties or suits. But they are still expected to be ‘smart’ and, in a competitive world, finding the *right* kind of smart becomes its own nightmare.

Few people have the sense credited to Albert Einstein who had twenty identical black suits on the basis that life was too short to worry about what to wear. Meet him half way – wear loose clothes (unless you are scuba diving), sandals whenever you don’t risk foot rot on seriously wet days and stick to Number 23 at all times. Sorted.

Twenty one
Masturbate regularly

Johnny Rotten said that sex was just a 'squelch'. It is certainly a squelch that creates moralising zealotry around both the benefits and pitfalls. High on the pitfall list is masturbation, said to lead to impotence, madness, damnation and more. It's just possible that the only real threat to our souls in all of this is the amount of hypocrisy involved.

The 1860s were the high point of associating masturbation with insanity though the notion persists to this day.[1] For contemporary psychiatrists, onanism and masturbation are positioned as healthy – a release of pent-up frustration, a way of maintaining arousal in relationships (especially when mutual) and as a means to 'curing' erectile incompetence.

This inverts theories prominent in the nineteenth century while illustrating one way in which 'scientific discovery' tends more to a circular than a linear trajectory.

In the nineteenth century, the alienists

(psychiatrists) Rush in the USA and Esquirol in France regarded masturbation as pathogenic. Both invoked masturbation as a symptom of mania that might, among other possibilities, lead to vertigo, epilepsy and death. Since the 1960s, therapists have suggested this supposed pathogen as a treatment. This is perhaps the equivalent of offering in a few years' time cigarette-smoking as a cure to cancer sufferers or the recent proposal that cannabinol oil might relieve the so-called symptoms of schizophrenia; a reversal of popular theorising that smoking cannabis *leads to* psychosis.[2]

For the psychiatrist David Cooper, 'orgasm is a contagious, good madness.'[3] Cooper adds that orgasm is a political act; the five or so seconds before orgasm are the only time that we are lifted beyond the demands of capitalism. Coming is the only imperative.

Mutual masturbation may follow if you have a partner. This brings with it a considerable bonus – to paraphrase Woody Allen: 'Now you're having sex with *two* people that you love.'

Twenty two

Live with several different people including a Jew and a Catholic

If you have been to college or lived somewhere too expensive to afford renting singly, you've almost certainly already lived with several different people. It would be nice to think that this increases tolerance, but sometimes it will have just confirmed existing prejudices – if you were a phenomenologist, you'd say that that's the only way we see the world; we invent it based on existing schema as we go along. Well, with apologies to Husserl, Number Twenty Two is about opening yourself up to a different world-view.[1]

As every religion has many variants, you can't assume that Catholic A will be that similar to Catholic B; likewise Judaism, Hinduism, Atheism and so on. There will be some bottom lines worth exploring though; contraception, what the person means by G-d (or why the person puts a dash rather than writing the letter O for that matter), what the person thinks of paying interest, morality, the meaning of 'after life', and so on.

Then there's a bunch of rituals to get your head around. Working at a therapeutic community like The House of Affirmation (a New England centre for priests and nuns who had gone off the rails) was an eye-opener. Some of the priests were alcoholics so, rather than having wine at communion they had blackcurrant juice. This is true faith; it's not wine that is magically transmuted into the blood of Christ, it's Ribena™.

I had already lived with a Catholic by then – he would have found the Ribena™ stuff odd, yet entirely in keeping. After all, if communion can turn wine to blood, blackcurrant juice shouldn't be so difficult.

Since then, another good Catholic, to whom this book is dedicated, has demonstrated a quiet form of faith by example. It takes all sorts.

I wasn't raised Jewish. My mum's mother had married out and, apart from the occasional Yiddish word, got on with being what in the 16th century would have been known as a *converso* – not that she didn't act like a stereotypical Jewish matriarch.

When her goy husband brought his mates round on shore leave during the Second World War, her house became a (free) hotel for all and sundry. Did her generosity when I lived with her as a child influence my practice as a clinical psychologist? I did my best to be available to staff, created a trust fund (from earnings as a lecturer and expert witness I was entitled to retain personally) that provided both a library and psychotherapy training for staff throughout the organisation, ensured service recipients were paid well for their role on interview panels long before other National Health Service departments followed suit, organised a staff counselling service and gave money to patients.

No doubt the last would be regarded as a terrible breach of 'boundaries'. As chair of the Psychotherapy Section of the British Psychological Society, perhaps I was leading the way. Freud believed in payment as part of the contract to the extent that he loaned money to the Wolf-man to pay for his analytic sessions – with Freud.[2]

Beyond that, my version of Judaism has elements of early Jewish thought. G-d is, quite literally, life. So we are all G-d, as are trees, breathing animals and the rest. Worshipping G-d is tricky and comes laden with all sorts of clutter – for Maimonides there are 614 *mitzvot* (duties).

But worshipping life? What else is there?

Twenty three
Don't bother with underwear

Can you name the most sensual thing you have seen or heard? *Paris* is Malcolm Maclaren's legacy. Hard to find now, it is a full-blown love letter to the city. A salacious beginning with his highness declaiming words that even the libertarian Zappa may have deemed *de trop*, is followed by glorious, glorious music encompassing gentle jazz, an African chorus (*Anthem*), extraordinary drumming and – wait for this – both Françoise Hardy and Catherine Deneuve on vocals.

You half expect Jane Birkin to show up; *Je t'aime* is there but in MM's inimitable style, so no Gainsbourg. No Edith Piaf either, but Miles gets a mention.

The Deneuve track includes a moment of genius. She is encouraged to sing: 'Sing away, Catherine'. In halting English – perhaps the sexiest voice ever committed to vinyl – she declines, her questioning, 'Sing away?' echoing for a few bars. And then she does, indeed, sing and this questing, pale

Englishman has conjured up a never to be bettered intensity from this beautiful French siren.[1]

But … In *Prick Up Your Ears* there is a scene when the playwright Joe Orton (played by a beautiful, slim Gary Oldman) is about to go cruising. Just before he leaves his lover Kenneth Halliwell (played by Alfred Molina) in their shared apartment, he takes a moment to take off his Levis, then remove his underpants. Halliwell is devastated and Orton heads for a local public toilet.[2] I was 33 when I saw it and haven't troubled with underwear since.

It's a suggestion you might find, what? Obscene? Absurd? Somehow distasteful and, if a woman, possibly unclean? Imagine going to a Cognitive Behavioural Therapist who suggests you keep a diary of your thoughts for a week writing down the evidence for their accuracy as you go. CBT doesn't work – not least because people don't *want* to be constantly reminded of their miserable thoughts by writing them down – to say nothing about the fact some people think in colours or sounds, not words.[3]

Now picture taking your underwear off and never bothering with it again. Which would you rather do?

Twenty four
Go fishing and decide for yourself if it's cruel

It is.

This doesn't mean that you can't eat fish. Sartre talked of Good versus Bad Faith. As Socrates said: 'An un-reflected life is not worth living.' Knowing that fishing is cruel while you tuck into fish and chips means you are in Good Faith. Obnoxious though it may seem, a politician who knowingly lies about an expenses claim is in Good Faith, unlike a person who walks out of a pub without paying for their drink and justifies the theft on the basis that the pub is making too much profit – the thief is still a thief.

Eating fish will also give you the opportunity to learn how to fillet them, another skill to develop; always use a fish knife and sharpen it every time you do:

She leans back against the dresser watching him work;

sharpening the fish knife. 'How can he bear to do it that way round with the blade drawn fast and efficiently toward his left hand holding the steel?'

He lays the knife down and begins to de-scale the fish; a saupe. As he delights in telling her, it is half the price of grey mullet, itself half the price of red. The fish is meaty too, a steely grey. But it first needs de-scaling with a clever studded implement bought for the task. Then the gutting, de-finning and the rest.

Filleting saupe isn't as straightforward as the fishmonger makes it look. For the red-faced man behind the iced slab at the shop a fast downward slash away from the head on each side and voilà! Two sizeable fillets.

She has noticed that he prefers a more careful approach inserting the blade into the flesh by the dorsal bone. 'Dorsal!' he had said. 'That's good!'

'Well even I know it's not called a backbone, Mister!' Then he slices away from the bone, gently negotiating the blade's path across the ribs to the underbelly now lying flayed on the board.

The process repeated, both fillets are placed on a plate while the remaining bones are added to the pan. Leek, carrots, fennel and whatever herbs he has foraged join the mix along with a litre of water and voilà! *Ten minutes of hard boiling later the stock is allowed to steep until deemed ready.*[1]

Twenty five

Know that so-called psy experts make it up as they go along

There are, officially, around four THOUSAND psychological theories of personality. There are many, many more world-wide, ranging through countless religions, folk wisdom and family mythologies. The thousands of official theories compete or complement each other and rise and fall within popular discourse.

For a time in the early years of the twentieth century, it looked like Freudian notions of the unconscious would conquer the industrial north but soon multiple analysts came up with ideas about child-hood, the importance of symbolism, parenting, you name it. And the behaviourists were soon to herald entire theories based on observable conduct, rather than mysterious inner worlds. Within fifty years, every sub-branch of psychology was exploring the importance of brain biochemistry, genetics, unconditional positive regard and so on in attempts to pin-point that elusive entity, personality.

But that is but one example of the nonsense that psy professions push in their own search for meaning, cultural capital and financial gain. There are over six hundred therapies[1], no reliable evidence that any of them work for more than a few weeks[2] and so many psychologists have been found to be corrupt, tainted by explicit value systems quite alien to science (the promotion of the Aryan ideal by Jung, for example[3]) or simply lying – that the whole basis of modern psychology and psychotherapy is shaky indeed.

Psy professionals, quite literally, make it up as they go along. They are bound to; in the consulting room, for example, it is not possible to predict what the patient may say next and it is beyond either the patient or the psy expert to work out the influences behind what they might say or do. Despite the claims by professional bodies to be well registered, licensed and regulated, none of this can tell any given professional *why* they prefer this theory to that or *why* they focus on one utterance rather than another.

This is because the distal influences on our lives

(culture, native language, promotion of theories by publishers, researchers and drug companies with massive vested interests, earning power, global climate change, etc) are – by definition – too distant to grasp. Which is why the proximal influence of family, the height of the therapist, the smell of the room, the perceived authority of the psychologist are positioned as of most importance. And again, even these aspects (height, family of origin) are unchangeable, so focus tends to move towards those things that appear close at hand, for example, the particular theory the therapist is leaning on or their qualifications.

But they don't know. If they did, psy professionals would be markedly more rounded and healthy than the general populace. And we're not.

Twenty six
Write something every day

Funny how many people claim to have 'a novel inside them'. What they mean is that they have had an interesting life. But having a novel 'inside' is no use at all. The only way to write is to – er – write. Keeping a diary is good enough; something we tend to abandon as teenagers.

Diaries give us an idea of who we once were, sometimes not so far removed – other than in time – from who we are now. A diary from 1978 informs me of the addresses of all the London embassies – now defunct Czechoslovakia is there, shortly followed by both the German Democratic Republic and the German Federal Republic. The Soviet Union precedes both the Yemen Arab Republic and the Yemen Peoples Democratic Republic.

The address section reminds me that I was living in Onslow Gardens, not far from the notorious murderer Dennis Nielsen and includes telephone numbers for Jasmine, Ully, Nick Davies and John Mullin, whoever they might be.

An entry for 27 September includes the line: 'Stanley Clarke (bassist) could well save my life' and a snippet cut and sellotaped in from what was probably the letters page of the *Daily Mail* reads: 'I would like to say how much I have enjoyed Mary Whitehouse's talks on *Thought for the Day.* At this time, when the morals of our youth in England are at such great danger it is time we had some straight talking …' *(Mrs) Irene Godfrey, Worthing Sussex.*

What would Mrs Godfrey have made of the legalisation of cannabis and internet porn? These moments would have been lost without writing the diary…

Don't fret about getting your jottings into print or on a blog. You are trying to develop a habit, not fame. Publication comes through luck, contacts, learning how to write book proposals, possibly getting an agent… It's hard work. So, start with developing a habit. You can use pen and ink, pencil, lap-top, whatever.

If you do manage to get yourself published then you will live a very long time. The human body takes about thirty years to rot; publications kept in the vast vaults of the British Library last three hundred as a minimum. *Beowulf* is over a thousand years old and it's not even in the vaults.

Don't expect to make any money. You're not JK Rowling or Nick Hornby. But you can take hints and tips from your favourite author. Try writing with no punctuation or capitals, try verse (Auden said that a poet was someone who couldn't manage decent prose), blank pages are good (have a look at the first modern novel, Laurence Stern's *Tristram Shandy* that appeared in 1740) and, unless you have an amazing memory, keep a notebook with you to record what you see and hear. Good writing comes from observation. There you go – all set. Write down the next conversation you overhear and you're off.

Twenty seven
Respond quickly to letters and other correspondence

Doesn't sound so hard does it? Most of the people reading this will probably think: 'So what, I do,' and move on. It's not like correspondence is unusual in these days of texting, Twitter, Messenger and the rest. For many people, response is as close to instantaneous as we are likely to get – which is part of the problem. There's no time for thought or more strategic (devious?) replies and one element of communication - the command aspect - is lost in a swirl of rapidly typed words.

For those not familiar with 'command', as it applies here, it's a term often used in family therapy. According to the theory all communication has two components – content and command. The first is factual; 'That's a chair' is simple enough when pointing at an object you sit on. Now try. 'THAT'S a chair!' or, 'That's a *chair*?' Implicit in the emphasis, stress and punctuation you can perhaps detect pride, criticism, sarcasm and more. Much of this kind of communication requires the speakers to be face to face or on the phone.

In the days before digital media reduced most of us to instant feedback junkies, people had to think about what they might put in a letter and be careful to say what they meant and mean what they said. So, responding *quickly* to letters was harder. Likewise, before pay-online became the norm, it was important to keep some stamps handy in case that final-demand suddenly appeared with a one week deadline.

As an editor receiving up to five new articles every week, responding with a simple: 'Ta, I shall send your submission for review' ensured there was no back-log of material to wade through every month. 'Clear Your Desk' might be the kind of notice people would pin to the wall as a reminder that unanswered mail just becomes a drag. If you don't already have the habit of responding quickly and thoughtfully to correspondence, have a go at it. As a new habit it has the advantage that letters and lengthy emails are becoming a thing of the past, so your recipients might sit up and take notice.

Twenty eight

Send greetings cards more haphazardly

This fits neatly with the previous ways to change. If you are adopting a lengthier style of correspondence or writing a regular diary, then you can give yourself a break from some of the more automatic ways of communicating with people.

You can buy books whose sole purpose is to remind you when people's birthdays come around and the number of special days for sending cards to 'show that you care' will soon outnumber non-special days. Do yourself a favour – if you have one of those birthday books, get rid of it. If you don't you are already ahead of the game. The next step is to give yourself a YEAR off from sending greetings cards.

Er, that's it.

Twenty nine

Play a musical instrument at least five hours per week

'Information is not knowledge, Knowledge is not wisdom, Wisdom is not truth, Truth is not beauty, Beauty is not love, and Love is not music. Music is THE BEST.'[1]

It used to be said that Keef Richards slept with his guitar. Perfectly understand-able if you are half way through that latest riff and Mister Sandman calls. Stuck near Torremolinos around forty years back with a guitar left back in England twenty four hours previously, it was time for action.

Oddly, Torremolinos, whatever its reputation for red-skinned Brit debauchery, has a fantastic luthier. So, the equivalent of £250 pounds later and anyone close to the villa could hear House of the Rising Sun all night long (as it happens '*All Night Long*'[2] was a few years away). Wind forward to 2006 and I'm researching – and describing – the awesome fish market in Vigo, soon to feature in

Tearagh't.[3] But, it's pretty much the same story; thirty six hours without a guitar and this minstrel is bereft. A few hours later in the hotel room, an electro-flamenco is awaiting its first experience of the blues.

See what I mean about life-changing? I started playing (kind of) guitar over fifty years ago. It took three years of constant practice before the switch from A minor to F was easily accomplished (and another thirty before Bb6 to F was fluid enough to include in a self-penned song). But in all those years, there was something to look forward to – learning a new tune, writing a few[4], playing with different bands, just hammering out a few songs for the cats' entertainment …

Like playing a sport, the appreciation of music is enhanced one-hundred fold if you can do it yourself, albeit less professionally. Segovia, Julian Bream, Zappa, Lucinda Williams, Steve Vai, the Boss himself and Sir Keef all increase in stature if you know how difficult this stuff is.

'Where am I going to find the time?' you may cry. The middle classes call eating in the middle of the day lunch. But, they don't need to eat then – it's not as if they are facing five hours of back-breaking labour in the afternoon. So, if you have a job that gives you thirty minutes break in the middle of the day, take you instrument with you. Easier still if you work from home.

There's also an immediate ambition for any instrumentalist – to be better than you were yesterday. *Couéism* (a form of self-suggestion popular in the 1920s) rested on the bland assumption that repeating 'Every day I am getting better and better' would somehow produce improvement.

You want to improve? Then *actually* improve at something – playing guitar, piano, mouth organ, trumpet, whatever. If you go for guitar you may need to stop biting your nails which will count as *two* changes in one.

Result!

Thirty
Don't try to be liked

People get themselves into all sorts of knots thinking that they should be liked and bend over backwards to behave in different ways with different people, according to what they assume the other person will like.

Somehow, being liked is no longer an aim just for dependent children and teenagers who want to have more friends than anyone else. If your aim is to be liked, you might get a shock when you discover that the things you *expect* to be liked for aren't held in the same esteem by many people other than you.

Facebook comes closer to reality than some may realize in the 'being liked' game. You can get an emoji for something you put online. Just like in real life, it doesn't matter at all whether the emoji sender thinks you believe whatever you posted, what is being 'liked' is what you have said. You are being rewarded for what you do (smile, flutter your eyelashes, grimace, cry etc), not what you *are.*

There's even a song you can sing to yourself as

you abandon trying to be liked. The band Sandghosts[1] gets requests for it. All the verses are made up according to who happens to be in the audience but the chorus doesn't change: *You don't see me. / You just see the one you think I used to be….*

Thirty one
Celebrate friendship

My friend Dorothy Rowe (Ooo … get him! That's such a Dorothy-esque way to name-drop; you may have to look her up if you are under fifty) used to say that friends were more important than family because you get to choose your friends.[1]

That rather assumes the existence of choice (a development of the increasingly consumer-oriented nineteenth century) rather than the alternative, that we just do what we do. It's a viewpoint offered by David Smail (another friend), who saw people as being influenced by close (proximal) and distant (distal) power.

The proximal influences are fairly easy to see (an approving look from a parent, a sudden burst of cold air leading to putting on a jacket, etc) but distal forces (culture, language, family myths, etc) are so embodied in who we are that the influence is mostly invisible to us.[2]

As a compromise let's assume that friendship chooses us. And when it does, celebrate it. As often and in as many different ways as you can. This is where Number Four comes into its own. This household celebrates Burns Night, New Year, Channukah, Christmas, Valentine's night, numerous birthdays and, for thirty five years, Thanksgiving.

It's a time for friends, for memories of friends and for welcoming new people around the table. Vegans and vegetarians will need to be catered for and the turkey ordered in September (this is very confusing to some butchers who will assume you want it for Xmas). This was last year's menu:

Thanksgiving 2018

Trump - the turkey

Pilgrim parsnip gateau

Blair broccoli bomb (anyone)

Crazy red and green cabbage

Clinton carrots

Mighty mash

Putin Peterloo pumpkin potato

Syrian shallots

No wall Mexican red bean and spinach delight

Stuffing everyone

Snake oil sauce

Russian raita

Cranberry crusade
Very (not beri-beri) Berry Apple pie
Mrs May's Brexit meringue
Calming collaborative cheesecake
Peaceful pecan pie

Enjoy.

Thirty two
Search out solidarity

PCCS Books published *This is Madness: A critical look at psychiatry and the future of mental health services* twenty years ago.[1] Half the contributors were survivors of the psychiatric system, all the contributors – including the professionals – were sick of it and were looking for some kind of solidarity struggling with an oppressive system.

But, solidarity doesn't have to be for a grand political cause. You will need some kind of help in pursuing any of the Ways you don't already do. This is because you may meet some resistance, especially when it comes to numbers One, Two and Thirteen. The early months of Number Twenty Nine are unlikely to be a breeze either.

Independence is the great goal for many people but what we need is mature dependence – knowing who you can trust. Joining Alcoholics Anonymous has proven useful for thousands of people. The changes outlined in this book could need a similar sponsor or, better still, group.

The simplest example is learning to play cards. If you are a beginner, seek out a local card playing group. Bridge is popular though you might prefer Bezique just to add a note of mystery.

The solidarity will help with any resistance back home and you are sure to get some. We live in a world of habit and living with someone else requires a development of mutual habits (some good, like sharing the cooking, some bad like always having a row before you go out). All of the Ways involve developing new habits and these may throw anyone you live with out of sync.

So, find some people to help you along the way. If the person you live with is up for it, get them to join you in change. For Number One, that's essential.

Thirty three

Run, swim or cycle and play something competitive (cards will do)

See Number Three if you have any interest in why I started running, but all the Ways are really a testament to physical survival and, to run, you need to be pretty fit. As I write this, I happen to have a blood pressure device that tells me that my low resting heart rate is 49 as it has been for many years. Perhaps it's genetic happenstance, perhaps all those years as a teenager going swimming training in the North Sea off Great Yarmouth beach – in winter!

Any of the first three in this Way will require persistence and some sweat. The second doesn't require a pool or fearsome gym membership costs – the sea is good enough. Rivers too, if you happen to be close to one that isn't too polluted; one reason for doing Number Fifty One is if the foreign country you are off to is France. Cycling will require a bike, the less fancy and expensive the better as you need to struggle a bit.

After her husband walked out, the family matriarch (see Number Twenty Two) lived with a survivor of the trenches. Like her ex-husband and herself, 'Uncle Joe' could play cards seriously well. The Ex had made a bit of money playing cards (and mandolin) during his time on the Mediterranean merchant ship convoys. The new lodger didn't smoke, so he had made a small fortune playing cards for tobacco rations during the First World War; men will gamble a lot if they think that today will be their last.

The outcome of all this card-play was a family packed with people who played – everything from Newmarket to Euchre via Bridge, Solo and Pontoon.

You may not have this kind of back-ground or maybe you gave up playing Rummy or whatever as a teenager. But cards, like running, swimming and cycling can be both a team game (Bridge) and hone a competitive edge. Playing cards happens to be a pretty cool way to interact with children and grand-children.

It was cold that Christmas. Snow everywhere. Too cold to go out much and the vans didn't come every day – just too icy. We played cards – euchre. We feasted on fish for Christmas Eve and then woke up to champagne on the day itself.[1]

So, why are you waiting?

Thirty four
Do as many chores as you can when going from one end of where you live to the other

Do you get the sense that the Ways don't seem to offer much in the way of relaxation? Don't worry. If you starting your running, swimming or cycling regime you'll soon be sleeping like a log. This one is more about filling time with something useful.

And if you live with someone else, I'm sure they'll appreciate the effort you put in. It's said that women are trained to see dust (it's a dictum that has been taken up by all sexes in this household except the writer) and, I suppose, at a pinch if you are sick of doing the chores then you could apply the opposite approach and just down tools. More time to crack on with reading those Dickens novels (Number Seven) or possibly an opportunity for Number Twenty One.

But in the spirit of hard slog (come on, hoovering is hardly working down the pit is it?) this Way is better than most for schooling yourself in systematic planning. Because you'll want to do these chores (that may be no more than putting a glass on the drainer) as efficiently as you can. Chores aren't called chores for nothing. They are a pain – the bigger the house, the bigger the pain. Likewise the greater the number of non-adults or adults not helping you run your home like a military operation, even more pain. It would be surprising if anyone reading this has servants but, perhaps you are lucky/rich/idle enough to have the modern equivalent – a cleaner. That means you can skip the cleaning element of fulfilling this Way but, to be frank, if you drop out cleaning, what else is there? Apart from watering plants, doing the washing up, re-touching some paint-work, replacing a light bulb, re-arranging the house plants to get the best light/shade, fixing that puncture, weeding …

Thirty five
Use ordinary words, not technical labels, to describe how people behave

A couple of definitions. A technical label is one that has some form of authority or expertise backing it up. Conduct is what people *do*. It will be some kind of behaviour. What distinguishes us from other animals is often seen as the moral dimension to our behaviour – that's what makes it conduct.

Technical labels to describe what we do and feel are more common than you might think. 'Anxiety' for example, is used instead of 'fear' and 'depression' instead of feeling overwhelmed (or *opp*ression which is more accurate). It's probably hard to keep in mind that these words were originally technical terms invented by the psy industries.

Using them has benefits – you might feel a bit lighter if a GP tells you that your fear and avoidance is a disease (Generalised Anxiety Disorder). You may feel less responsible for hiding away and you can probably claim personal independence payments from the state. Drug companies will make a profit from the pills you are prescribed, your partner might be a bit less hard on you and, if a rambunctious child is inscribed with ADHD and given Ritalin, a primary school teacher may get some peace.

But the notion of moral agency has vanished in all of this. What's it about? Is it time to get a grip?

Modern professionals, including psych-ologists and psychiatrists, tend to act as if their knowledge results from the accumulation of many years of trial and error, history inevitably leading us to a new enlightenment.[1] It is difficult to remember that any knowledge is little more than a way of emphasising (privileging) certain ways of seeing – ways that serve their interests rather than describing immutable truths.[2] So-called post-modernists can imagine they are in a meta-theoretical position, kind of above it all though, as Iris Murdoch asked: 'What follows post-modernism?'[3]

A technocracy such as psychology will emphasise ways of seeing the world, and those within it, which can be measured. Such measurement may take the form of quantifying assumed internal characteristics (intelligence, introversion, depression) of individuals. Hence the popularising of computerised Cognitive Behaviour Therapy (CBT) for those whose conduct can be conveniently divided into discrete, de-contextualised chunks of thought, emotion and behaviour; each chunk to be then separately modified with the aid of a computer programme.

In a parody of the scientific method,[4] the people psychologists see have already been branded via psychiatric diagnoses. Arbitrary and unrelated behaviours have been observed or reported before being clustered into seemingly random concepts – depression, schizophrenia, etc. This sleight of hand obscures the fact there is no reason that, say, visual hallucinations or voice-hearing should be investigated as part of the same syndrome, yet psychiatric researches set about looking for a single cause (genetic or bio-chemical) or various interacting causes (environment, up-bringing, genetic predisposition, etc.) underlying the diagnosed malady.

Since its inception in 1952, the Diagnostic and Statistical Manual of the American Psychiatric Association (DSM) increased the defined diagnoses from a mere 162 to (in the year 2000) 365. DSM5, released in 2011, had the same number. By then, *all* human behaviour had been covered – so we're all mad.

For the animal world, Jose Luis Borges suggested a different form of categor-isation: those which have just knocked over the water pitcher and those which from a distance look like flies, beasts owned by the Emperor, and so on.[5] It is possible to imagine a similarly challenging typology of persons, less reductionist and more visible, than that currently embraced by psychiatry, psychology and related professions.

A walk along a crowded beach in summer can give us a starting point. We might categorise people in the following, less technical, ways: those that play with children, those that show off their bellies (tanned or otherwise), those that can balance a football on the back of the neck, those that scream as they run into the sea, and more, *ad infinitum*.

Such ways of seeing people can be developed in more subtle and equally easily verifiable ways. Let us continue: those that regard history as a biased account of the past, those that see G-d in everything, those that understand planting rhythms, those that smoke to change their consciousness (albeit briefly) and those that do so out of habit, those that prefer touch (healing) to talk (mouthfuls of air[6]), those that prefer giving to receiving oral sex. The list is endless.[7]

You may have a psychiatric or psychological label. You may be claiming disability benefits or taking drugs based on your label. Perhaps, you picked up this book in the hope of finding an alternative way out of things.

It will sound harsh, but your next step is to stop using the label to describe the conduct of yourself or other people. It's quite a challenge; you can't move an inch without some sports star or TV personality declaring that the reason they did such and such was because they were 'depressed.' You, like them, will lose an excuse for your conduct but then you'll be able to do something about it. As I said, it's harsh – but real.

Thirty six
Avoid physical fights

'May you never lose that your temper of yours,
If you get in a bar room fight.
And I hope that you never lose your woman overnight.'[1]

Are you training to be a boxer or kung-fu expert? Skip to the next one. This book isn't about rules (unless it's about breaking them – see; Number Twenty One). Nonetheless, there are a couple of guidelines for fighting. Verbal fighting can be good (Radio Four listeners tend to call it 'discussion' or 'debate.') and struggling (with the latest recipe, cycle trip or cross-word, for example) is grist to your mill.

But, if you insist on struggling with someone else, stick to verbal pugilism with a couple of rules. Whatever numbers Thirteen and Nineteen say, limit yourself to shouting when alone or swearing in the nicest way possible if you're having a verbal spat.

If the tempers rise, you may find yourself justifying shouting with reference to something akin to passion. My grandmother convinced my mum that the shouting she witnessed as a child was a sign that her parents really loved each other. My grandfather duly left and mum was left with a rationalisation of all the rows she went on to have with my dad.

If it turns physical - see Number Two. If you are in a bar with strangers, just don't do it.

Thirty seven

Don't make happiness an ambition

The US Constitution may preserve the right to *seek* happiness, but no-one has a right to *be* happy.

The desire to escape pain and fear has been with us a long time. More recently, perhaps, there is a growing desire to escape boredom in a techno-world so accelerated beyond our capacity to govern it that a few moments contemplation can seem an eternity.

Just as movie car chases must become faster and more dangerous, perhaps the perpetual white noise of an industrialised world's need for speed has increased such that an exhausted majority seek oblivion through alcohol and licit and illicit drugs.

We live in a world of celebration of the self or families and 'friends' on Facebook, supposedly joyous rituals like marriage, the birth of a new child to a 'happy couple' (particularly when that couple is famous or a member of the aristocracy), finding employment, 'succeeding' in getting a university place and so on.

These events are meant to bring 'happiness' to ourselves and those around us. But, of course, a perusal of divorce, unemployment or debt statistics shows how Facebook posts and other celebrations are, like happiness itself, transitory. (No doubt, US readers will dismiss this as a view based on a rather gloomy European intellectual and philosophical tradition – they're right.)

One impact of the promotion of the pursuit of happiness is a mismatch between our feelings and what we are told we should feel; a married woman with a good career, university education and new baby simply shouldn't *be* unhappy. It can be a short step to inscription and entry into the psy system.[1]

'I just want you to be happy' is a common refrain of a parent witnessing a child struggling with exam nerves or on the sports field. However kindly meant these words can be taken as an instruction. Suddenly the child has a far more complicated target – happiness.

Happiness is transitory and only sometimes comes from the kind of things that are meant to bring it as a reward. Number Seventeen (Appreciate the glory of the night sky), for example, is unlikely to bring happiness as part of appreciating the night sky is understanding how irrelevant we all are in the universe – not a happy thought for many.

Number One (Get rid of your TV) should bring some relief as well as the time to do follow some of the other Ways but you may experience a *frisson* of loss next time someone asks you if you caught such and such the previous night. And some people will think you are mad. So, don't go for happiness, go for survival with the occasional grin.

Thirty eight
Live somewhere for ten or more years

You will have gathered by now that some of the Ways are connected. *Living somewhere for ten or more years* may help you achieve several of the Ways like searching out solidarity, joining a club or supporting your local school. It might not, however, be on your current agenda. So what are the advantages?

First up is the length of time it takes not to be known as the 'new people'. Myddle has the distinction of being the first ordinary place to be described in detail – housing, population, births, deaths, occupations, friendships – in an English language book.[1] *The History of Myddle* was first written in 1701 and there are families in the book whose descendants still live in the village (and you thought it was the monarchy that just went on generation after generation). Ten years is no time at all in Myddle, but a little of that 'new people' aroma will have gone after a decade.

Next up; if you are serious about growing vegetables (Number Ten), it takes a while to learn about soil, planting cycles, light, shade and the rest. Ten years should do it.

Don't get alarmed – the other four Ways (see: Introduction) are still available to you, even if staying put doesn't feel like much is changing. There's always Number Forty Five to be used as a get-out clause.

Thirty nine

Eat by candlelight regularly

As ever, this is far easier said than done. After all, who wants candles lit if you are eating in front of the telly? Mind you, if you are trying Number One, the telly will be gone. Unless you live in an old people's home or other institution.

In his discussions on Death-making Wolf Wolfensberger wrote of how institutional life is *designed* to kill either the body or the spirit.[1] It's all done in the guise of help – labelling (frequently with a psychiatric diagnosis), drugging, living with other people that no-one wants as they are a burden or too troublesome.

The buildings are part of the death-making paraphernalia, especially fire doors that are simply too heavy for frail people to open unaided. Now imagine insisting that you should eat by candlelight most nights – rules about fire procedures would have to change, artificial lighting would have to be dimmed, and so on. But the atmosphere would change – and so would you and the staff.

Now picture it in your own home. There is something *softening* about candle-light. Perhaps you would argue less with a partner. Perhaps, if you live alone, you would be gentler with yourself.

I have eaten by candle-light for over forty years; privileged to be sure as I don't need permission to do it. I suspect it has contributed to Numbers Three, Four and Ten (to say nothing of Eighteen and Forty four).

If your only experience of eating by candle-light has been in restaurants, then maybe it's time to learn to cook so the restaurant comes to you (you won't even need Deliveroo).

Forty

Spend time with someone who is very, very ill with cancer

Some years ago, I came across an article on the desirability of moving clinical psychologist expertise into the world of the cancer sufferer. The article was brief and well referenced. These references included the *Journal of Psychosomatic Research*, the *Journal of Psychosocial Oncology*, the *British Journal of Cancer*, *Cancer Surveys*, *Social Science and Medicine*, the *Journal of the Association of the Society of Clinical Oncology*, *Psychological Medicine* and the *British Medical Journal*, all, no doubt, prestigious examples of the scientific approach.

My partner had recently received a secondary diagnosis of lung cancer. Neither she nor I sought solace or information in these journals. I didn't need to. I had already read, some 20 years before, Solzhenitsyn's *Cancer Ward*. I knew that visits to hospital would be marked by waiting alongside grey-faced, anxious people and their forlorn lovers and relatives. I knew that the wards would be terrible places where emaciated people would barely glance up as we came in and side rooms would be reserved for the middle classes and the dying.

I had already known, like Solzhenitsyn's Aysa, the moment when a breast would be offered up for kissing one last time as, 'Today it was a marvel. Tomorrow it would be in the bin'.[1] And I knew all this at 15.

I can't remember the authors of the article on clinical psychology and cancer but *Cancer Ward* stays with me still. As does Douglas Dunn's poem, 'Second Opinion', in which the narrator notices, with understated envy, the wedding ring of the junior doctor tasked with breaking the news of his loved one's spreading cancer.[2]

Perhaps you work in a cancer unit – I take my hat off to you. Perhaps you have already cared for a loved one with cancer. Worse, perhaps you have been wracked with guilt while caring for someone you hate with the same disease.

News reports are filled with stories of people courageously facing a lingering death from a disease that spreads and spreads – not just through the person, but through the family, neighbours, friends and beyond. Living with someone with a terminal illness is harrowing and can result in some rivetingly honest exchanges – as well as regular visits from Macmillan nurses or emergency services and trips to the local hospice.

If what doesn't kill us really makes us stronger, then I guess these experiences are strengthening. Certainly, howling at the stars in despair is a form of catharsis.

I don't recommend you find someone with cancer with whom you then live – but watching someone die a protracted death will certainly change your life. You might even have some steroids and morphine left over to ease things a little.

Forty one
Be on time for people in and out of work

Foucault (1975/1977) cites the Gobelins school (established via an edict in 1667) as the first documented guild – where '...domestic service is mixed with a transference of knowledge.' (p.156)

It is the start of 'the development... of a new technique for taking charge of the time of individual existences.... The disciplines, which analyse space, break up and rearrange activities, must also be understood as machinery for adding up and capitalizing time.' (p.157)

Also: 'The disciplines function increase-ingly as techniques for making useful individuals.' (p.211)

By the mid eighteenth century, the schools 'became a sort of apparatus of uninterrupted examination that duplicated along its entire length the operation of teaching...a perpetual comparison of each and all that made it possible to both measure and judge.' (p.186) The Brothers of the Christian Schools, for example, wanted pupils to be examined on every day of the week; on the first day spelling, the second arithmetic, the third for catechism and handwriting and so on.

More than that: 'The examination that places individuals in a field of surveillance also situates them in a network of writing; it engages them in a whole mass of documents that capture and fix them.' (p.189) 'Hence, in order to extract from bodies the maximum time and force, the use of those overall methods known as time-tables, collective training, exercises, total and detailed surveillance.' (p.220)[1]

Ironic that in instituting a system for disciplining the uneducated and uncontrollable peasantry and military, it is just such internalised discipline that enables the modern independent doctoral candidate to succeed, bankers to work until they drop, surgeons to work through the night, nurses to work extra shifts due to staff shortages, teachers to spend whole weekends writing lesson plans[2], on and on…

Being on time is an aspect of discipline, not always as good as it sounds. After all, I was on time to pick my friend and colleague up only ten minutes before the accident that changed everything. If, however, you are tardy and a little lax when it comes to turning up for appointments and assignations it's time to develop a less anti-social habit.

Forty two

Alternate between the main newspapers – but focus on the cryptic crossword

Old hat now, newspapers, but they're all available online. The posher ones have cryptic crosswords. They have a language all of their own and if you are up for Number Fifty One, they are a good place to start. If you buy the printed version it's worth knowing that *The Daily Telegraph* also makes excellent material for the base of a log fire.

As you already know the 'news' isn't news at all. The people involved already know what's happened, interviews are plugs for books, films and new music and some papers – take *The Daily Star* (please) – are filled with adverts for money-lending, usually by the same company that owns *The Daily Star*. In between the half page photographs and quarter page adverts you will find any number of press releases, all produced by companies with something to sell but, be patient, towards the back you will find a cryptic crossword.

There should be some kind of award for crossword compilers. Check out the cross-words around Xmas – the clues and answers are inspired versions of Yuletide celebrations and the clues are *never* repeated, even between papers.

So, hats off to *The Daily Mail, Telegraph, Times* and *Guardian* and here's to three hours in bed with the Sunday equivalents. This is the beginning to learning a new language. Be patient – it will take some time to understand the codes but what a moment when you first get it! Celebrate.

Forty three
Join a club

Footie, books, political parties, bridge – they all have clubs. And it's about solidarity (see: Number Thirty Two) as much as anything else. There's a difference though. David Smail wrote about how intimate relationships (often between couples) have gradually become too demanding.

It's not good enough to face the world together and do your best to create a home. Now people are encouraged (those experts again) to demand that their partner be a friend, confidante, sexually satisfying, on and on. It's too much – hence the affair and divorce rates and the tidal wave of advice from 'relationship counsellors' in Sunday magazines or on TV.

But clubs aren't like that. Clubs have a mutual aim for members and friendship or shared confidences are a bonus. During a break you might get to spill the beans about your grim day at work but that's a distraction, however welcome.

Club membership also requires a degree of discipline. Going out on a cold and rainy evening to chat about the latest Jane Harper[1] might not feel preferable to curling up at home. It probably isn't. But just do it.

Forty four
Eat lots of garlic

This goes hand in hand with Number Four (unless you have opted to learn to cook nothing but cakes) and has an affinity with Number Thirty. Family therapist and philosopher Paul Watzlawick was famous for the axiom: 'You cannot not communicate.' In other words, anything you do or say will communicate something, silence during a discussion or argument being the obvious example.

Watzlawick also wrote *The Situation Is Hopeless, But Not Serious: The Pursuit of Unhappiness*[1] which includes a chapter, 'If you loved me you'd eat garlic.' The intent is only partly ironic and plays on the idea that people often use 'If you loved me, then …' before asking for something (perhaps the mutual aspect of Number Twenty One?). But garlic is well chosen here. For many people a garlic aroma is unpleasant – and the only way to get past a sickened reaction is to either leave the room or eat some them-selves. As Zappa said, so poetically: *A horny little Jewish princess With a garlic aroma that could level Tacoma.*[2]

Garlic is constantly promoted as health-giving; certainly the Chinese, Japanese and people living around the Med don't do so badly but their diets include a lot more than garlic so don't take up this Way as a route to health alone. Take it up as a way to get under someone's skin and, if they don't like the smell, plead: 'If you loved me you'd eat garlic.'

Forty five

If someone hurts you badly, run a long, long way

Being bullied as the only Yid in Grade 7 didn't offer much opportunity to run away. Like a battered house-wife, curling up and taking it was the order of the day. As for telling a teacher – forget it, that would have brought down more wrath.

But running away is fine if your partner hurts you. Get as far away as you can.[1] Perhaps go for Number Fifty One.

Forty six
Look after a dog, or dogs, for many years

People need structure. Retirees can struggle when they reach the longed-for day of stopping paid work. Animals and pets structure their owners' lives. Whether you're a farmer getting up every morning before sparrowfidget to see to the cows or a cat-owner letting your pet out at night, the animals' dependency demands that you arrange your day/holidays/availability around them.

Sounds too much like hard work? You could get a stick insect but even they need cleaning out.

A dog is a different, time-consuming, sometimes grubby, loyal, soothing, infuriating, demanding proposition. What's not to like?

Forty seven

Support your local community

Echoes of Number Thirty Two and potentially a first step towards Number Forty Five. Mostly, it's about being part of something and a real opportunity to learn.

Being a school governor is an eye-opener. In the nineties, a parent-governor group in Myddle discussed sex-education for eight year olds. It was all based on government guidelines – a few cross-sections of the reproductive organs and lots of stuff about the importance of relationships. Now, it's geared towards avoiding sexual assault and other harm and moralising about intimacy.

In the twenty five years that separate the ways the subject is approached, there seems to have been no room for the natural inquisitiveness of children or the possibility that some kinds of gentle exploration might be fun.

School governorship may not be for you but there are still people to help onto buses, laughs to share at the local WI and, if you are lucky, damsons to give away when the annual glut arrives. You see, it doesn't have to be *official*.

Forty eight

When you smoke dope, inhale

My mum tried her first joint on her 80th birthday. Memorable? Kind of – she unknowingly copied Ringo Starr who, when first given a spliff by Bob Dylan, smoked the whole thing without passing it on.

So I shouldn't be surprised when she was later asked why I didn't look much like either of my brothers and she informed the questioner: 'Different father, darling.' Dope can make you do that – in between the giggling (take a look at *Paul* for the ultimate stereotypic first toke[1]), sudden exhaustion and (hopefully) mild paranoia people are suddenly honest with each other.

The inhaling is all part of what *aficionados* call a 'hit'. Coughing and spluttering means you've got it. You won't get to the point of Shamanic dancing like Jim Morrison and you probably won't feel the need to move to Holland to investigate the coffee shop culture, but all sorts of movie scenes will suddenly make sense.[2]

Forty nine
Forgive your father

'The official Scots Guards version of the Malaysian Emergency tells a story of a successful if troubled campaign. In his introduction to *Noone of the Ulu* Field-Marshall Sir Gerald Templer's version is more upbeat. Doug Newnes, a regular soldier who served from 1948-1951 tells a different tale.

'In part this is his story, faithfully recorded by me in a series of discussions poring over a faded photo album. These talks are a tale in themselves: the story of a son and father who, finally, sat down to talk about the past. It's a past that shaped my dad, ours and countless other relationships within families of a certain generation – relationships with authority, G-d, queen, king and country.

'Of course, my dad's story also portrays a truth known to us all; that no one 'up there', be it in high command or the government, either knows or much cares what is going on for the rest of us. My dad learned that the hard way. May G-d bless him.'[1]

Forgiveness is unfashionable; revenge and

'justice' driven legal actions can bring compensation, profits to lawyers, book deals and, perhaps, a small sense of putting the past behind. If you are lucky there may not be too much to forgive. On the local bus, I met someone in her eighties who explicitly regards all but the last three years as blessed – privileged upbringing, rich parents, a kind dad and then marriage to 'the best man ever.'

For others there may be a history of violence, absence and cruelty, all of which is grist to the mill of therapists around the world.

I had it relatively easy. My dad was a philandering non-drinker who taught me to play football, told me to 'turn it down', taught me to ride a bike and was impossible to talk to, in part because he worked six to six night shifts and wasn't in the mood to ask about school for half an hour when I got home at 5 o'clock.

So I left home at seventeen with a powerful sense that half the problem was his age (he was 24 years older than me for G-d's sake, so what did he know?) and the other half his authoritarianism.

I had forgiven him long before we sat down to write a book about his part in the Malaysian Emergency and even found some of those qualities in him that made his few friendships last for over half a century.

But, who was he? 'Your real father, your historical father … is by no means the same thing as your archetype of fatherhood you carry in the depths of your being …'[2]

Fifty

Learn to drive

Take note, this isn't about owning a vehicle. This is about being *useful,* though the chances are you will want to own a car or equivalent; a shame as public transport, especially local buses, is a good way to meet new people.

If you learn to drive then you can give rides to non-drivers, hitch-hikers (don't worry, you are six HUNDRED times more likely to be murdered by the person you live with; so it might be a good idea not to give them a ride), your children, the people who have drunk too much as you fulfil Number Thirty One and all sorts of other opportunities to put some credit in the heavenly bank account.[1]

Fifty one

Learn a foreign language and live in a country other than that of your birth

Therapy is just a different form of linguistics. New words appear all the time – thoughts become 'cognitions', you may suddenly find yourself talking of 'projection', that 'inner child' might be playing up again and, G-d forbid, you might seek 'closure.'

Selflessness might be inverted as a bad thing or something to aspire to via 'mindfulness'. But, you can't do a lot with this vocabulary and therapists themselves use the words in different ways all the time. So, if you want a new language, get a real one.

It will take time and you will need people around who can share the excitement and mistakes as you struggle with pronunciation and unfamiliar grammar. This is where Number Thirty three will come in useful, but don't despair if you have skipped that one. There are still local language classes (filled with fellow strugglers – a form of solidarity) to use, as well as the occasional foreign holiday. Who knows? You might pick up a few words in Greek/Italian/Spanish/French *and* get a tan.

Again, the trick is practice. Comic books are a good way to start as they are mostly written for young people and have short and repeated sentences. You might be surprised just how much of that GCSE or O level learning is lying dormant. It still takes repetition. You need to get the mouth working as memory is in the muscles not some hidden part of your brain (it's why musicians can just do it without a thought).

Fifty two
Visit the Great Blasket

I shall give a small sketch of Coumenole and its vista. Off the south west corner of Irellande lie the Blaskete islands. These are home to a small and strangely independent community of families. An Blascoad Mor is the only island with housinge and shelter. Its fresh water allowes islanders to live, raise their families and work within view of the mainland (Coumenole is due North East from the Great Blaskete, about 10 leagues distance) with no need to cross the treacherous sounde in search of sustenance.

All around here the spoken tongue is Gael. Ffrench and Spanish are known - An Dingaen is a Spanish resort of sorts. The island families live by some fishinge, the raising of roote crops and a ceaseless supplye of gull eggs. The occasionale seal pup will find itselffe wash'd upon the strand where it shalle meet a quicke death at the hands of the island children – who knoweth a feast when they see one.

Beyond An Blascoed Mor (the Great Blaskete) lies An Tearacht, a terrible and lonelie rock that stands proud of the waves less than a cable high and perhappes ten across at yts base. Yt cannot be seen from the islanders' homes for they lie to the easterne lee of the Blaskete ridge. From a distance Tearagh't has a pinnacle that might appear the top of the most perfect mountain. From there to the West lies nought but oceane.[1]

The Blaskets are remarkable. Going due west from Tearagh't the next landfall is Newfoundland (though for centuries it was believed that the land of Bysse lay somewhere in mid-Atlantic). The world has many remarkable islands. But one that has produced numerous biographies written by islanders and now translated into dozens of languages? Countless copies of *An t-Oileánach (The Islandman)* by *Tomás Ó Criomhthain* (often translated as O'Crohan) have been sold since Robin Flowers helped Tomas to write down tales passed on via generations of islanders.

Published in 1929, it was soon followed by volumes from other islanders telling stories of a life so primitive by standards of the day that the reading public was torn between a romantic vision of a new Utopia and the terror of living in a place where getting to the main-land, not a mile distant, could be impossible for months on end.

Whatever you make of the Great Blasket itself, the curve of the horizon and the possibility of seeing up to five distant storm systems might give you pause…

Coda

The reader might see this volume as an exercise in hubris – as if the author could possibly know the factors that gave him a second chance. As for controlling cultural and familial influences … Born in 1954 to a Jewish mum keen on swimming and cycling, a Methodist dad who abjured alcohol and was a good footballer and devoted Ipswich Town fan, white, male, adored as the one that made it, first just *being* born (my mum had a boy before me who died after less than an hour), then being the one who excelled at sport and academic stuff (courtesy of an almost photographic memory and a mother who placed reading at the top of her list of 'things boys should do'), the first in the family to make it to university (in order to avoid the drudgery of being a ceiling tiler), on and on … all things beyond any kind of personal agency.

The 1950s in the UK was a time when people

were emerging from rationing, enjoying rock and roll, gazing in awe at Hollywood movies and, for some, getting on the property ladder. All sorts of restrictions were being left behind, television was replacing radio as popular entertainment and then … along came the 'sixties and unheard of freedoms for many.

Who knows which things were of most importance? Being white and male had certain advantages but jumping off a railway bridge and breaking an ankle? Was that more influential than hearing the Beatles for the first time and dedicating early adolescence to learning guitar?

Most elements of becoming a person before the road traffic accident in 2003 are absent from this account. How about respecting trees, getting to know a Palestinian, giving money to people who look like they need it … maybe next time.

But it's not an autobiography. The fifty two ways are simply some things you might do and if you don't have an accident as a focus for change, all the better.

Endnotes

If you don't really love the person you are living with as a partner, leave.

1. From: Newnes, C. (2016). *Tearagh't.* Steyning: Real Press p.215

Learn to Cook

1. From: Newnes.C. (2018). *Paris.* Steyning: Real Press p.289

Take the barest minimum of prescription drugs

1. https://www.webmd.com/drugs/2/drug-1836/effexor-oral/details/list-interaction-medication
2. BMA/Royal Pharmaceutical Society of Great Britain (monthly publication). *British National Formulary.* Oxford: Pharmaceutical Press

Always wear comfortable clothes

1. Bentham, J. (1843). *The Works of Jeremy Bentham,*

vol. 4 (Panopticon, Constitution, Colonies, Codification) p.39 http://oll.libertyfund.org/titles/bentham-the-works-of-jeremy-bentham-vol-4#lf0872-04_head_004 Retrieved March 19th 2017

Masturbate regularly.

1. Despite his liberal (though decidedly paternalistic) views on sexuality Havelock Ellis termed masturbation 'Auto-Erotism' and suggested it led to nervous disorders. In the second edition of *Handbuch der Sexualwissenschaften* by Moll he was recommending a masturbatory prophylactic - Onaniebandagen; suits of armour fitted over the male or female genitals and attached to a locked belt- first proposed by Lajade-Lafond in 1830. See; Marcus, S. (1966). *The Other Victorians.* London: Weidenfeld & Nicolson

2. https://www.medicalnewstoday.com/articles/317768.php Retrieved 3rd March 2018

3. Cooper, D. (1978). *The Language of Madness.* London: Allen Lane p.74.

Live with several different people including a Jew and a Catholic

[1] Husserl, E. (1913/1982). *Ideas Pertaining to a Pure Phenomenology and to a Phenomenological Philosophy—First Book: General Introduction to a Pure Phenomenology*, trans. F. Kersten. The Hague: Nijhoff

[2] Gardner, M. (Ed.) (1973). *The Wolf-man and Sigmund Freud.* London: The Hogarth Press

Don't bother with underwear.

[1] From: Newnes, C. (2018). *Paris.* Steyning: Real Press

[2] *Prick Up Your Ears* (1987). Directed by Stephen Frears Civilhand (UK)

[3] Otis, L. (2015). *Rethinking Thought: Inside the minds of creative scientists and artists.* Oxford: Oxford University Press

Go fishing and decide for yourself if it's cruel

[1] Newnes, C. (2018) *Paris.* Steyning: Real Press p.154

Know that so-called psy experts make it up

as they go along.

[1.] Feltham, C. (2013). *Counselling and Counselling Psychology: A critical examination.* Monmouth: PCCS Books

[2.] Newnes, C. (2016). *Inscription, Diagnosis and Deception in the Mental Health Industry: How Psy governs us all. Basingstoke: Palgrave Macmillan*

[3.] Masson, J. (1989). *Against Therapy.* London: Collins

Play an instrument at least five hours per week.

[1.] Cited in: Newnes, C. (2007). Frank Zappa (21 December 1940 – 4 December 1993). *The Journal of Critical Psychology, Counselling and Psychotherapy, 7,2,* 121-2

[2.] Richie, L. (1983). *All Night Long.* Motown.

[3.] Newnes, C. (2016). *Tearagh't.* Steyning: Real Press

[4.] Two CDs by Sandghosts and one by Cigarman are available via Spotify, Amazon or iTunes

Don't try to be liked

[1.] Tracks from the Sandghosts albums *Nine Moons* and *Villains and Fools* are available on Spotify or Amazon

Celebrate friendship

[1.] Rowe, D. (2001). *Friends & Enemies: Our Need to Love and Hate.* London: Harper Collins

[2.] Smail, D. (2005). *Power, Interest and Psychology: Elements of a social materialist understanding of distress.* Ross-on-Wye: PCCS Books

Search out solidarity

[1.] Newnes, C., Holmes, G., and Dunn, C. (1999). *This is Madness: A critical look at psychiatry and the future of mental health services.* Ross-on-Wye: PCCS Books To give an idea of the types of solidarity promoted in the volume, chapters include: Collaborative conversation – Peter Hulme, User involvement in mental health service development – David Pilgrim and Lesley Hitchman, The service user/survivor movement – Peter Campbell, Survivor-controlled alternatives to psychiatric services – Vivien Lindow, The duty of community care: The Wokingham MIND crisis house – Pam Jenkinson, Promoting community resources – Janet Bostock, Valerie Noble and Rachel Winter, The role of education in the lives of people with mental health difficulties – Tracey Austin and Green approaches to occupational and income needs in preventing chronic dependency – Brian Davey. This kind of collaboration isn't new; The Alleged Lunatics' Friend Society was formed in the mid-nineteenth century and there are now thousands of similar protest groups on Facebook.

Run, swim or cycle and play something competitive (cards will do)

[1.] From: Newnes, C. (2018). *Paris.* Steyning: the Real Press

Use normal words, not technical labels, to describe people's behaviour

[1] Calder, J. (2005) Histories of abuse. In. C. Newnes and N. Radcliffe (eds) *The making and breaking of children's lives.* Ross-on-Wye: PCCS Books

[2] Smail. D. (2005). *Power, interest and psychology*. Ross-on-Wye: PCCS Books

[3] Murdoch, I. (1992). *Metaphysics as a guide to morals*. London: Chatto and Windus

[4] Boyle, M. (1999). Diagnosis. In C. Newnes, G. Holmes and C. Dunn (eds) *This is madness: A critical look at psychiatry and the future of mental health services*. . Ross-on-Wye: PCCS Books

[5] Quoted in: Foucault, M. trans. A Sheridan (1971). *The order of things*. New York: Random House

[6.] Burgess, A. (1992). *A Mouthful of Air: Language and Languages, Especially English*. Harmondsworth: Penguin Books Ltd.

[7.] Taken from: Newnes, C. (2010). A non-toxic typology of folk. *The Journal of Critical Psychology, Counselling and Psychotherapy, 10, 4,* 228-231

Avoid physical fights

[1.] Martyn, J. (1987). May you never. From: *Solid Air*. Island Records

Don't make happiness an ambition

[1.] From: Newnes, C. (2018). *A Critical A-Z of Electroshock*. Steyning: The Real Press

Live somewhere for ten or more years

[1.] Gough, R. (1834/1981), *The History of Myddle*. Harmondsworth: Penguin Books.

Eat by candlelight regularly

[1.] Wolfensberger, W. (1987). *The New Genocide of Handicapped and Afflicted People*. New York: University of Syracuse

Spend time with someone who is very, very ill with cancer.

[1.] Solzenitsyn, A. (1968). *Cancer Ward*. London: The Bodley Head, p. 425.

[2.] Dunn, D. (1995). Second Opinion. In *Elegies*. London: Faber and Faber.

Be on time for people, at home and work.

[1.] Foucault, M. (1975/1977). *Discipline and punish: The birth of the prison.* New York: Random House. Quoted in: Newnes, C. (2018). Towards coherence in teaching critical Psy. In. C. Newnes and L.Golding (eds) *Teaching Critical Psychology: International perspectives.* London: Routledge. pp. 37-63

[2.] Piper, R. (2018). Fear and loathing in the education system. In. C. Newnes and L.Golding (eds) *Teaching Critical Psychology: International perspectives.* London: Routledge. pp. 82-99

Join a club

[1.] Harper, J. (2018). *The Lost Man.* London: Abacus

Eat lots of Garlic

[1.] Watzlawick, P. (1983). *The Situation Is Hopeless,*

But Not Serious: The Pursuit of Unhappiness. London: Norton Books

[2.] Zappa, F. (1979). Jewish Princess. From: *Sheikh Yerbouti*. Zappa Records

If someone hurts you badly, run a long, long way

[1,] So how far did I run? Hurt by my partner Jacqui living in what I thought of as paradise (North Witham, Lincolnshire), I fled first to Slough (hmmm…) and then to Boston, Ma. I was sacked by my first boss in Framingham who took a contract out on me when I threatened to sue (you couldn't make it up) and then was given a job at The House of Affirmation in Whitinsville (you couldn't make that up either, though it became famous in the film *Spotlight*). Re-united two years on we sped back to England and our daughter was from her mother's womb untimely ripped on 13 November 1987. Two years later and we were in Shropshire, Jacq had cancer and in 1996 was buried not a half mile away. Running away changes things.

When you smoke dope, inhale

[1.] *Paul*. 2011 film directed by Greg Mottola

[2]. Check out Johnny Depp's phenomenal take on walking into a casino after taking ether in *Fear and Loathing in Las Vegas*. Acting of the – er – highest order..

Forgive your father

[1]. From: Newnes, C. and Newnes, D. (2020). *Malaya: A kind of memoire.* Steyning: The Real Press.

[2]. Davies, R. (1972). *The Manticore.* New York: The Viking Press. Republished in 1983 as part two of *The Deptford Trilogy* by King Penguin. p.507

Learn to drive

[1]. Heavenly Bank Account. Song by Frank Zappa from *You Are What You Is* released by Barking Pumpkin Records in 1981

Visit the Great Blasket

[1]. From: Newnes, C. (2016). *Tearagh't,* Steyning: Real Press

The Real Press

If you enjoyed this book, check out some of Craig Newnes' other titles... at www.therealpress.co.uk